CW01332917

For free work sheets and activity ideas for this book, please email us at

sisters@holyassumptionmonastery.com

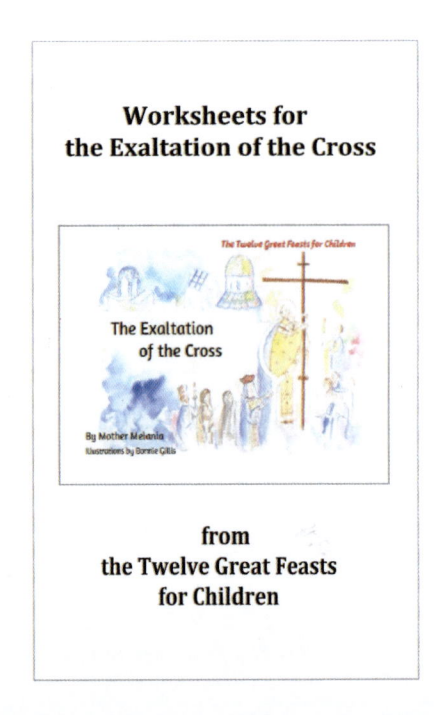

**Worksheets for
the Exaltation of the Cross**

from
the Twelve Great Feasts
for Children

Looking for Pascha (Easter) books?

Pascha at the Duck Pond -

A whimsical look at how to prepare and how NOT to prepare for Pascha.

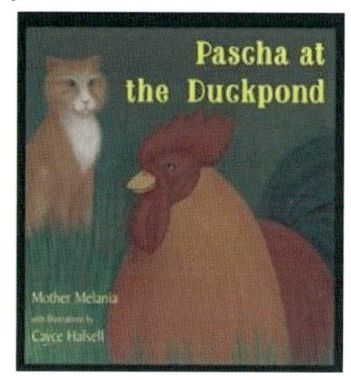

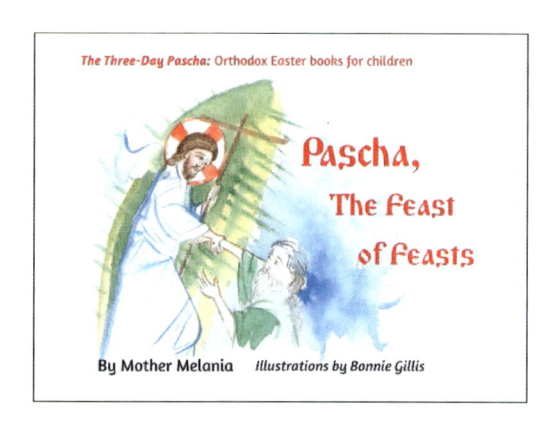

Pascha, the Feast of Feasts
from *The Three-Day Pascha series*

Be glad today! Be glad! Rejoice!
With all creation, lift your voice,
For Christ has died, but lives again –
Restoring life to fallen men.

The Exaltation of the Cross

from **The Twelve Great Feasts for Children**

Poems © copyright 2005 by Mother Melania
Illustrations © copyright 2005 by Bonnie Gillis

All rights reserved.

Published by Holy Assumption Monastery
1519 Washington St.
Calistoga, CA 94515

Phone: (707) 942-6244
Website: http://holyassumptionmonastery.com
Email: sisters@holyassumptionmonastery.com

The Exaltation of the Cross
from *The Twelve Great Feasts for Children*

by Mother Melania   **Illustrations by Bonnie Gillis**

(first published under her former name – Sister Elayne)

HOLY ASSUMPTION MONASTERY
Calistoga, California

THE TWELVE GREAT FEASTS FOR CHILDREN series:

In the Orthodox Church Year, the Feast of Feasts, in a class by itself, is the Resurrection. After the Resurrection in importance come the twelve Great Feasts. These feasts are the Church's celebration of, and participation in, key events leading to our salvation. The Great Feasts are often separated into Feasts of the Lord and Feasts of the Theotokos.

Feasts of the Lord
Exaltation of the Cross
Nativity of Our Lord (Christmas)
Theophany of Our Lord (Epiphany)
Entry of Our Lord into Jerusalem (Palm Sunday)
Ascension of Our Lord
Pentecost
Transfiguration of Our Lord

Feasts of the Theotokos
Nativity of the Theotokos
Entry of the Theotokos into the Temple
Meeting of Our Lord*
    (Presentation of Christ in the Temple)
Annunciation
Dormition of the Theotokos

* The Meeting of Our Lord is also considered a Feast of the Lord

A final note - Theotokos, an ancient title for the Virgin Mary, means "birthgiver of God." Used since at least the third century, this title guards the truth that Mary's Son is not only fully human, but fully God.

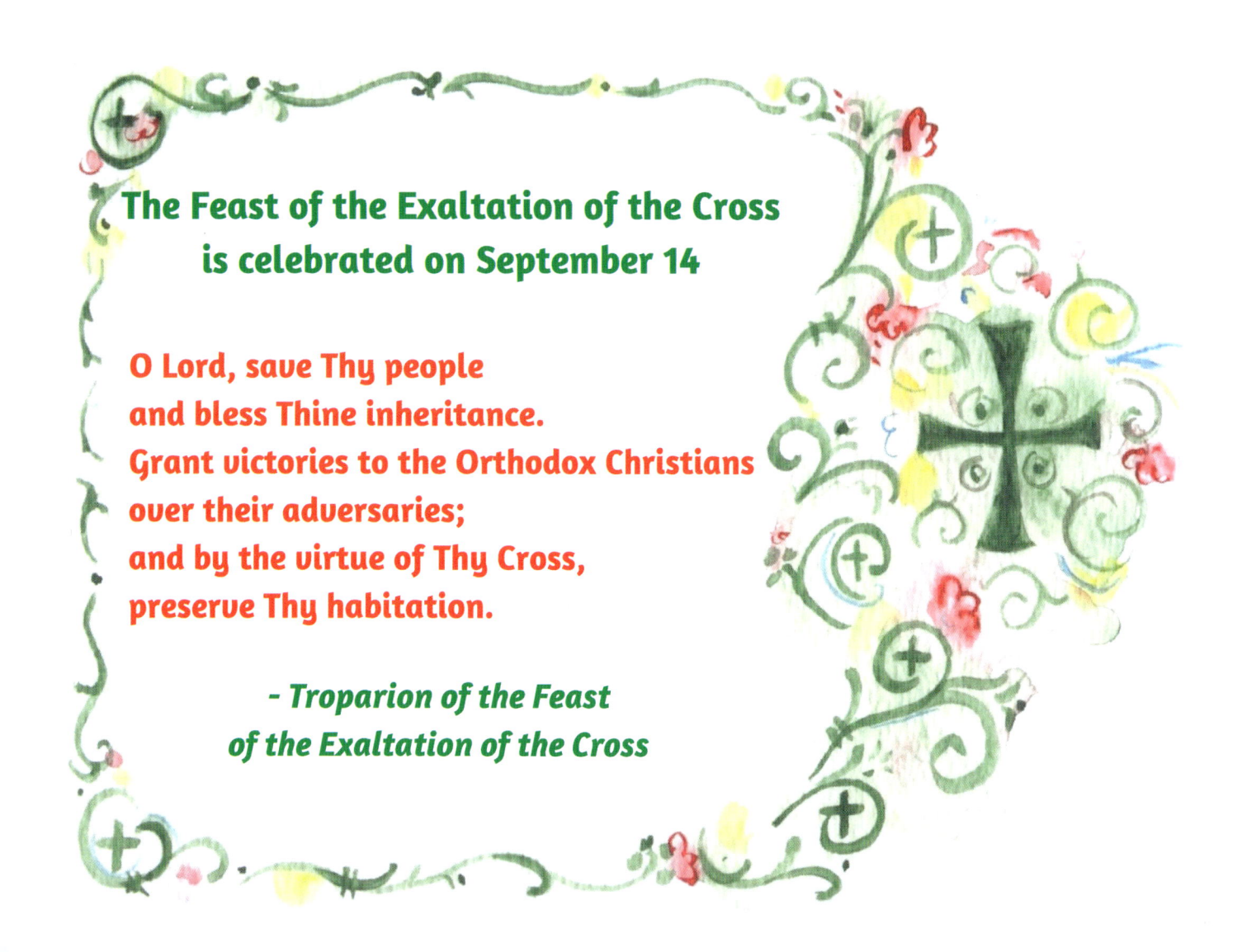

The Feast of the Exaltation of the Cross is celebrated on September 14

O Lord, save Thy people
and bless Thine inheritance.
Grant victories to the Orthodox Christians
over their adversaries;
and by the virtue of Thy Cross,
preserve Thy habitation.

*- Troparion of the Feast
of the Exaltation of the Cross*

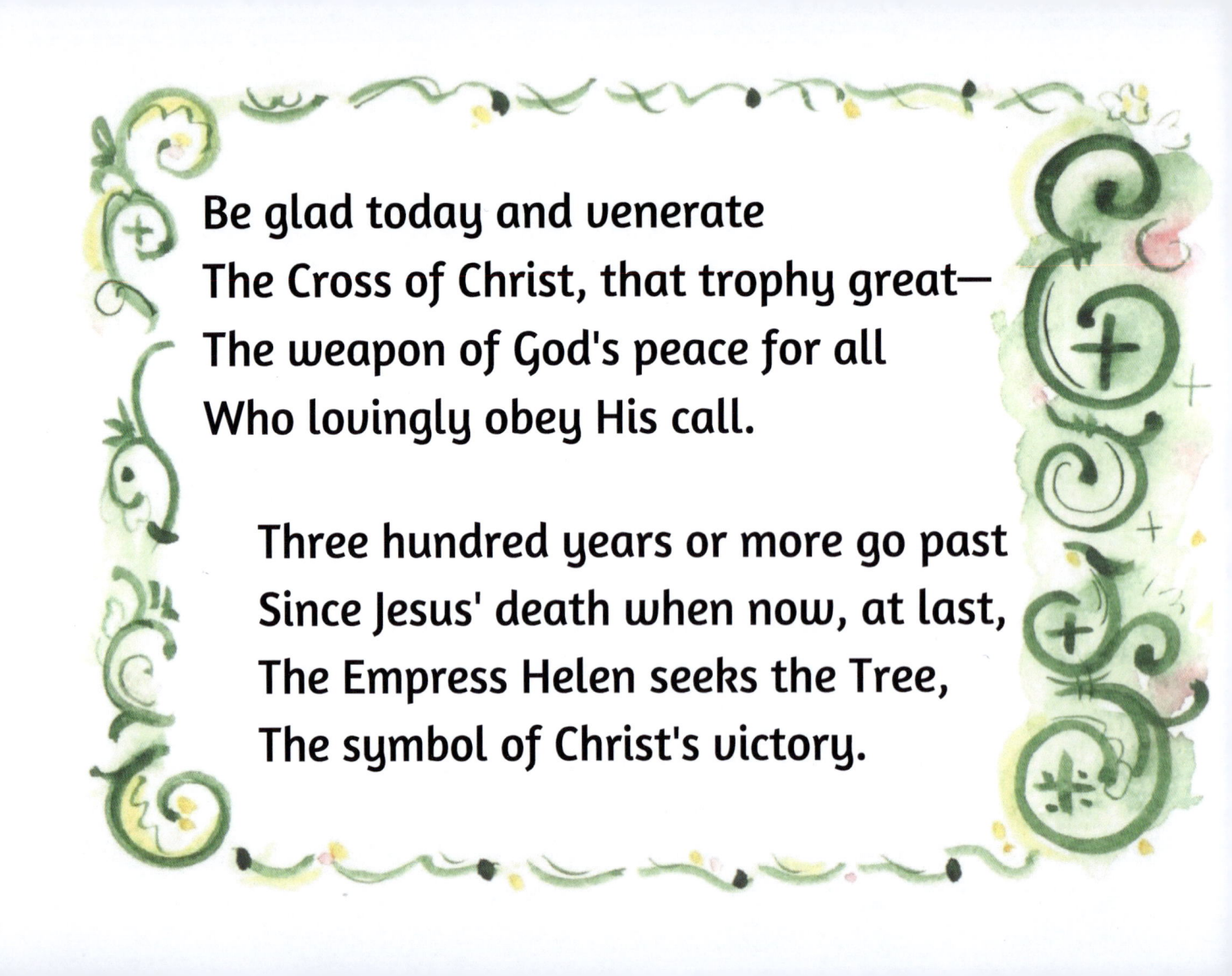

Be glad today and venerate
The Cross of Christ, that trophy great—
The weapon of God's peace for all
Who lovingly obey His call.

Three hundred years or more go past
Since Jesus' death when now, at last,
The Empress Helen seeks the Tree,
The symbol of Christ's victory.

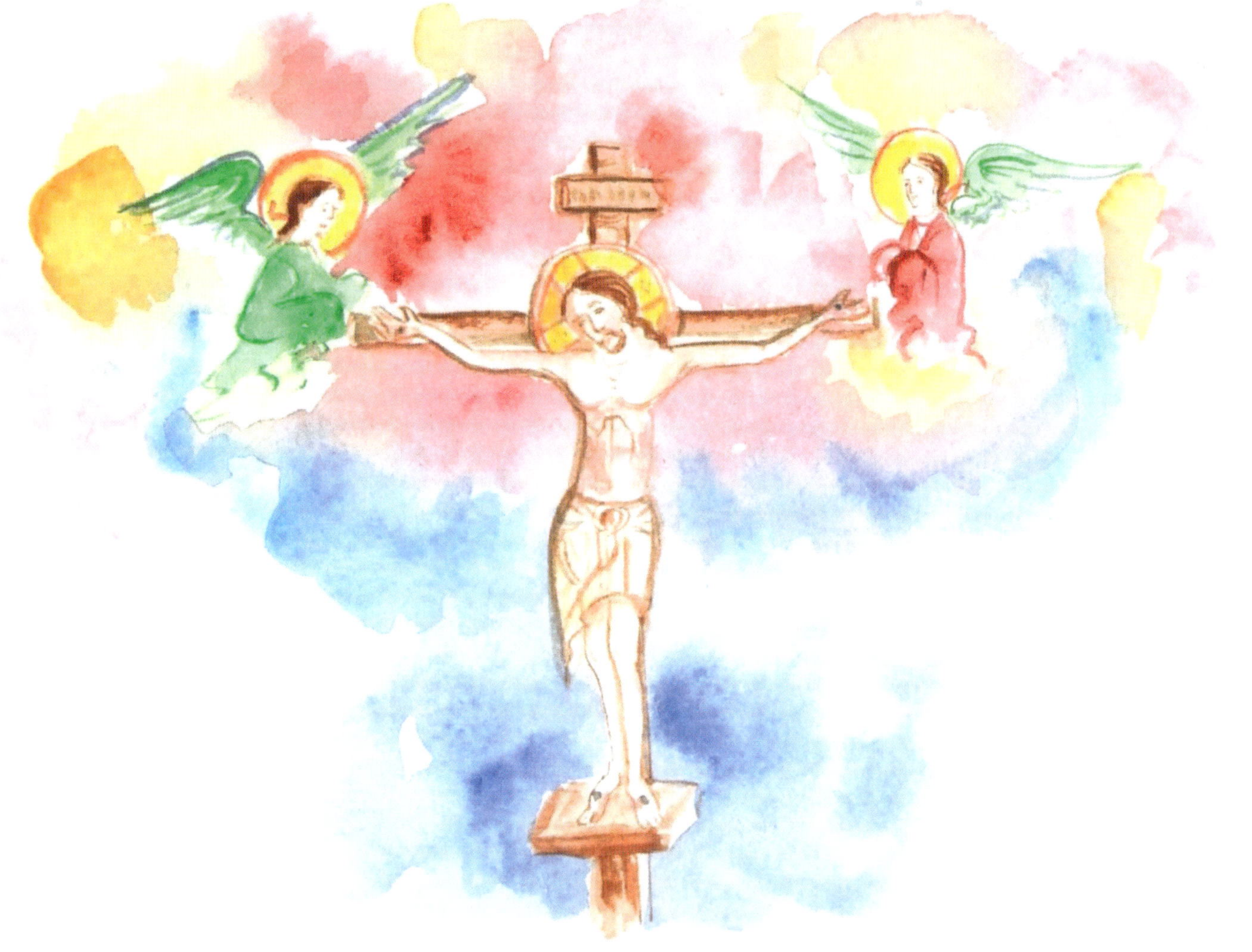

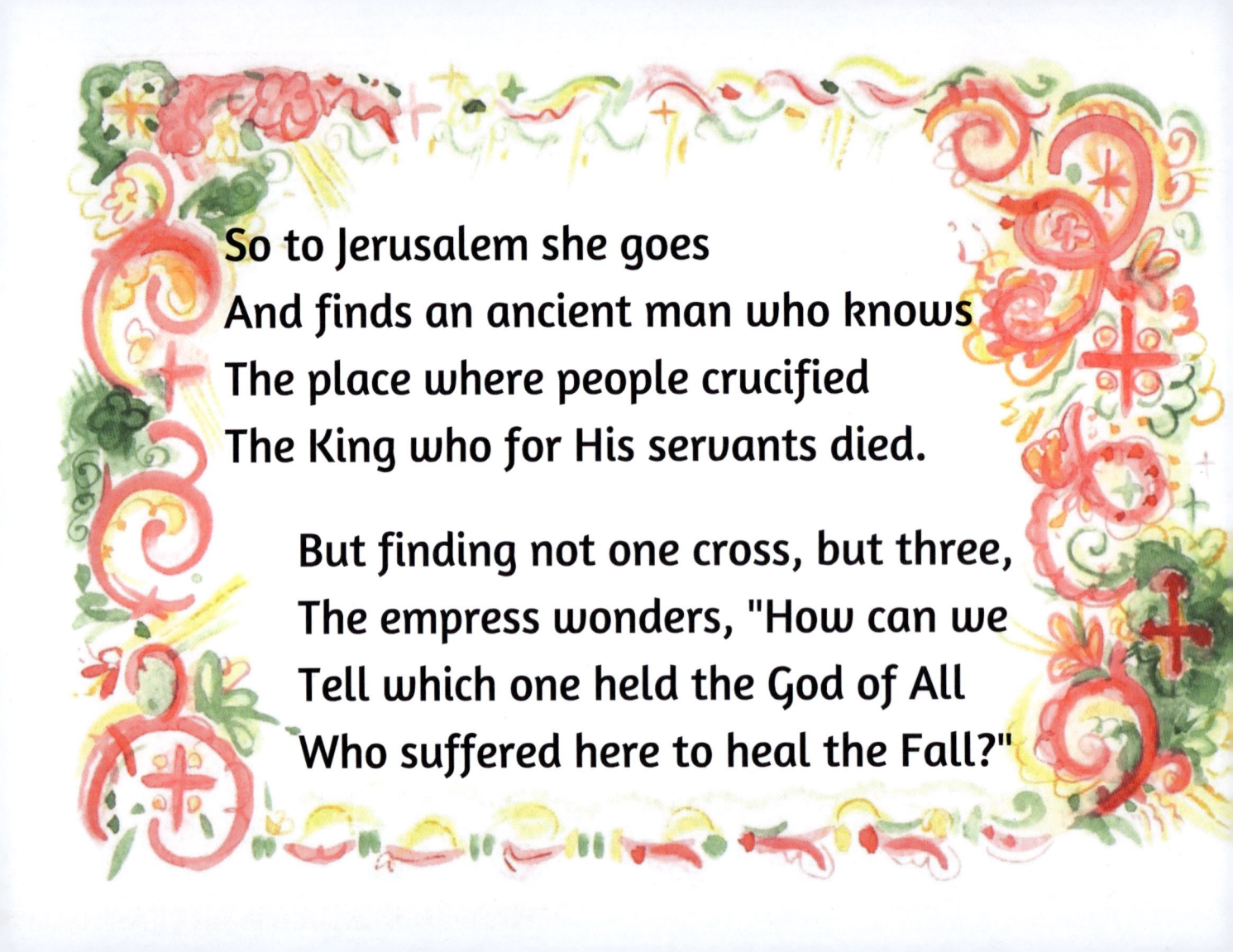

So to Jerusalem she goes
And finds an ancient man who knows
The place where people crucified
The King who for His servants died.

But finding not one cross, but three,
The empress wonders, "How can we
Tell which one held the God of All
Who suffered here to heal the Fall?"

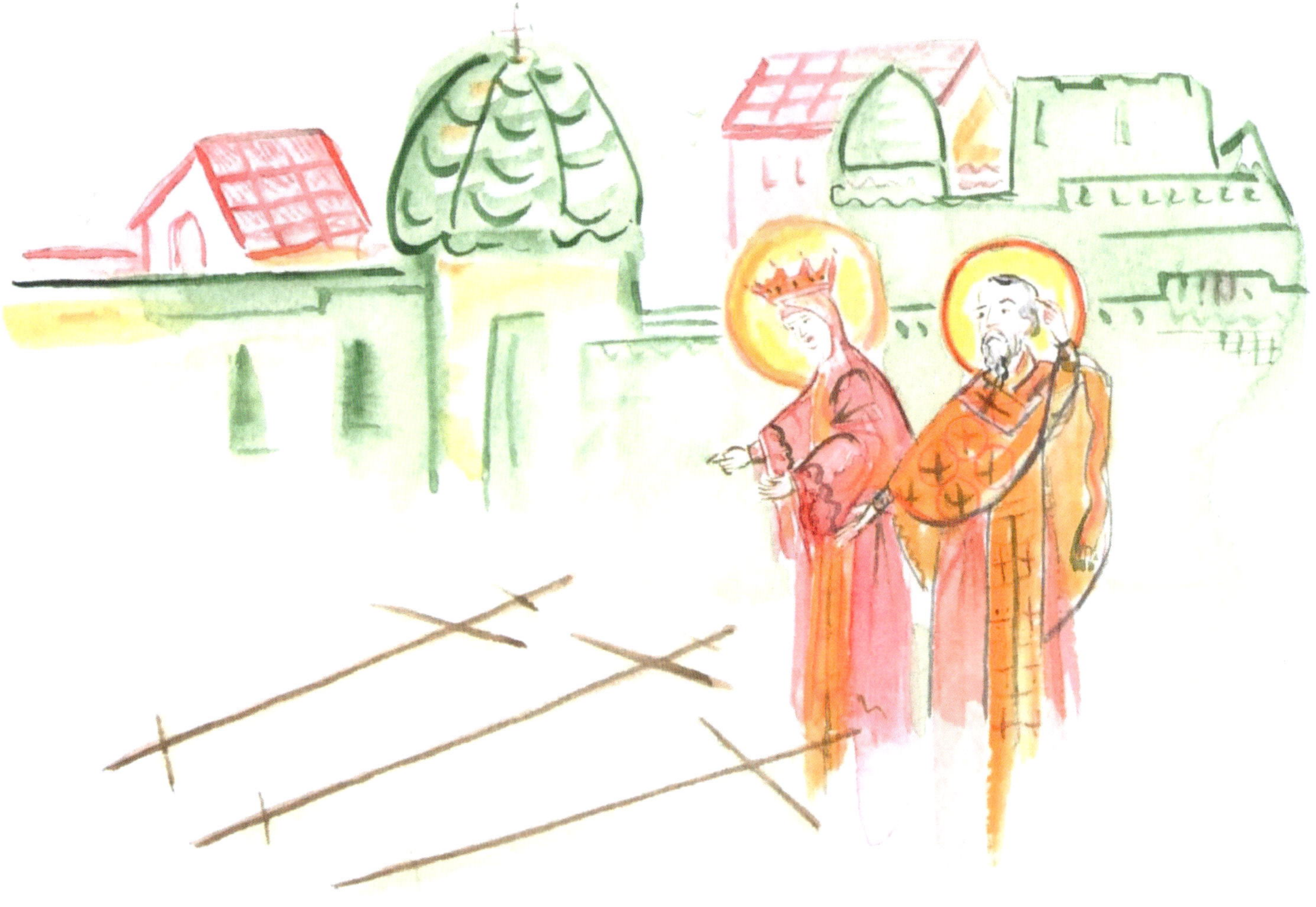

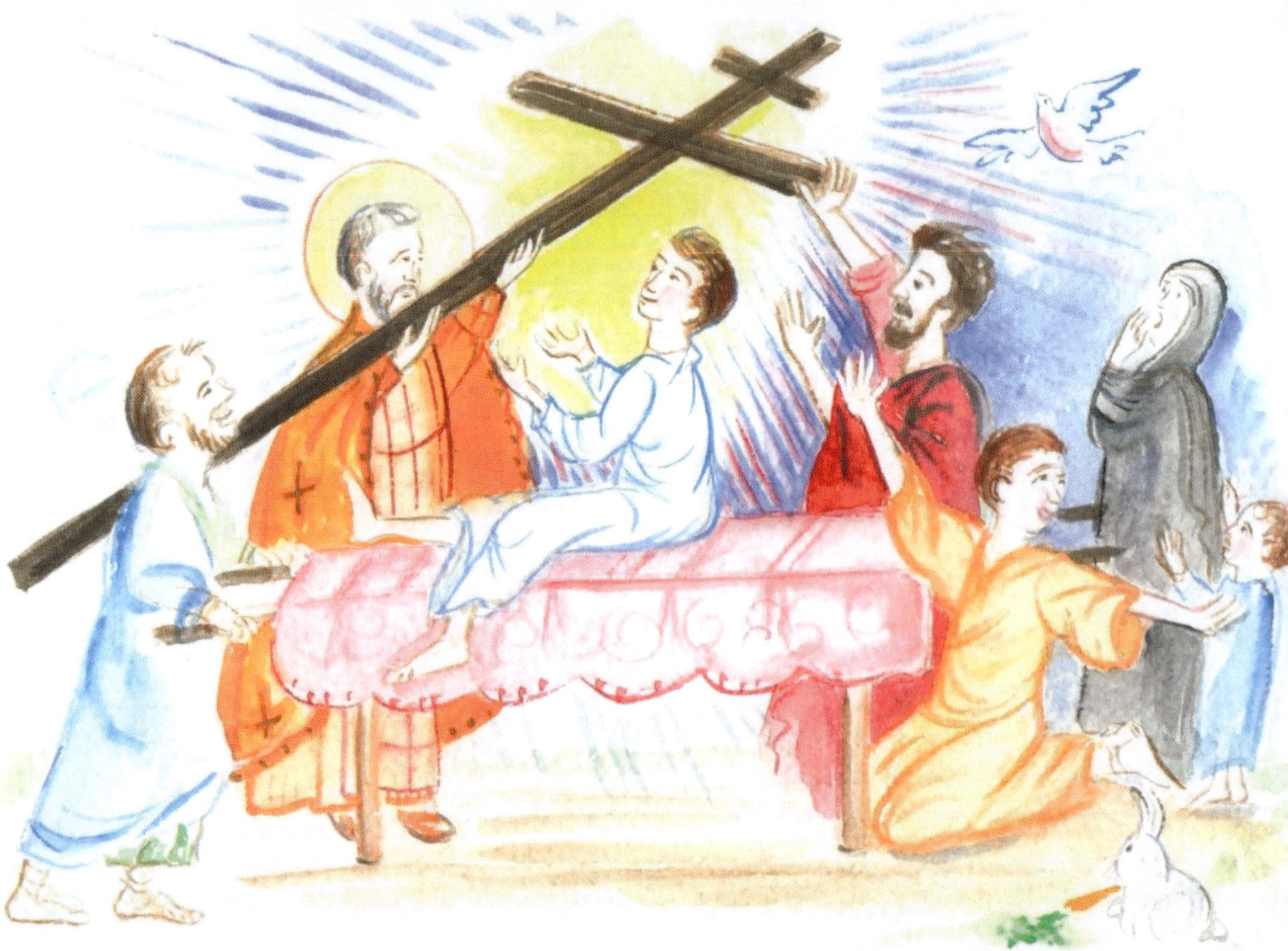

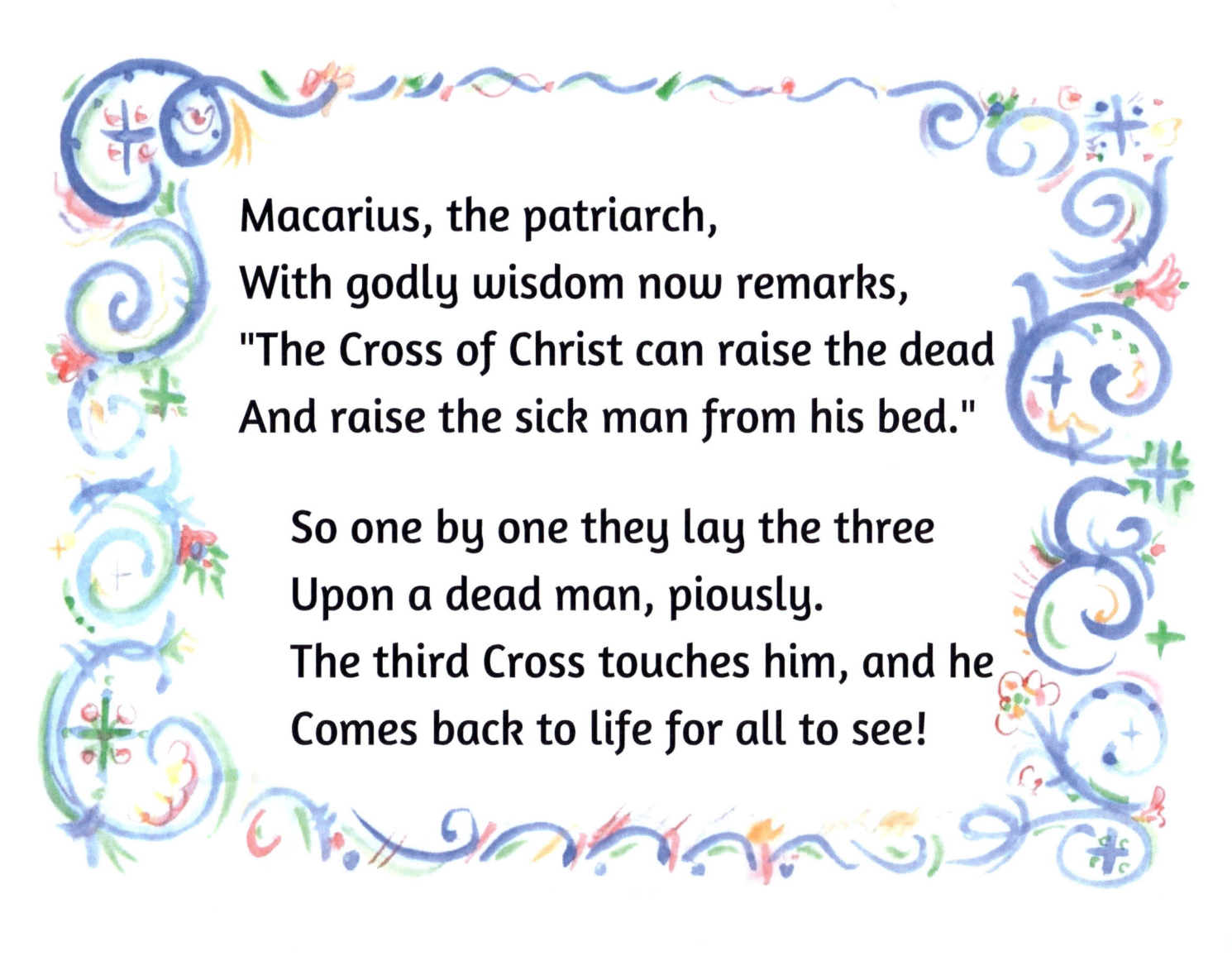

Macarius, the patriarch,
With godly wisdom now remarks,
"The Cross of Christ can raise the dead
And raise the sick man from his bed."

So one by one they lay the three
Upon a dead man, piously.
The third Cross touches him, and he
Comes back to life for all to see!

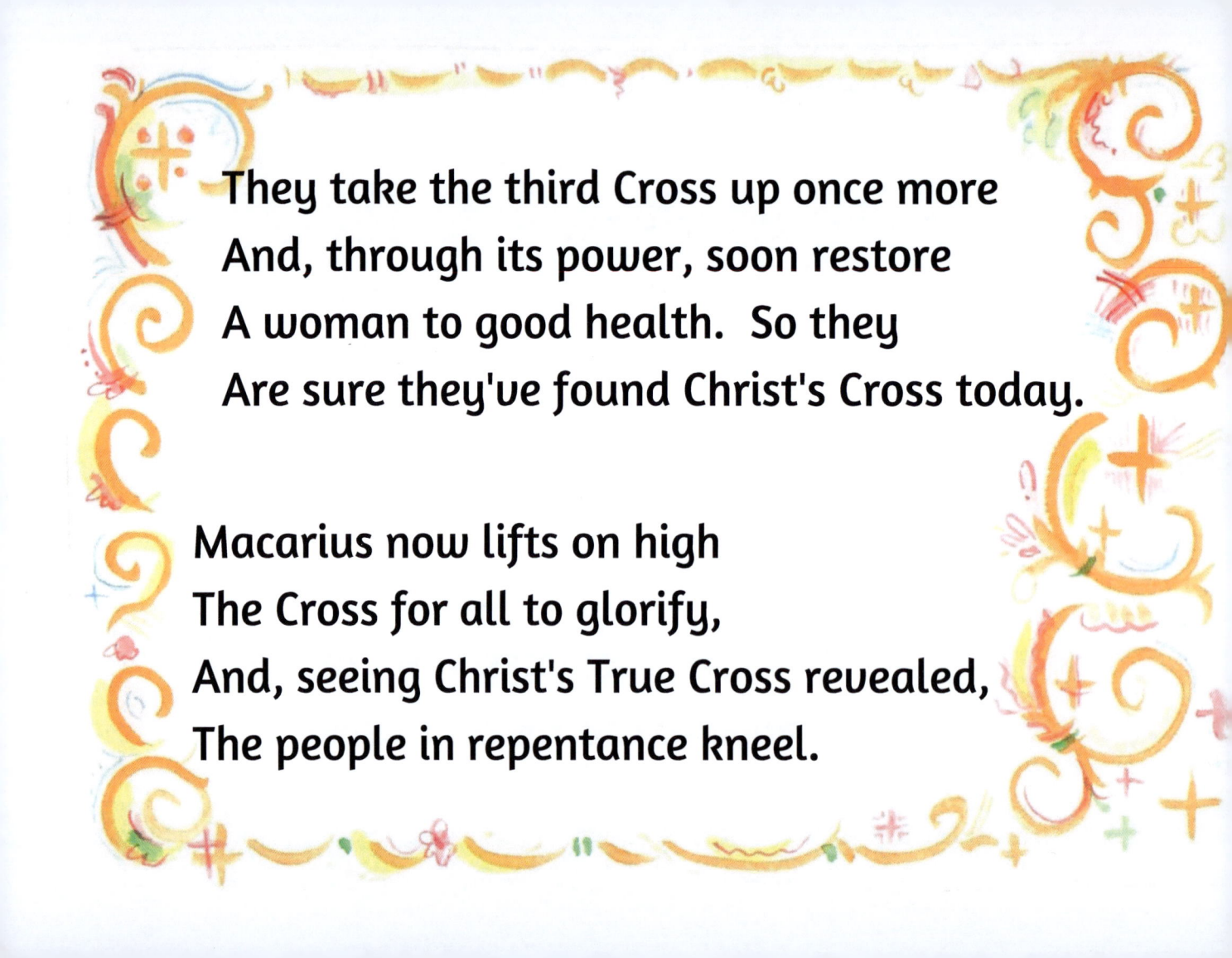

They take the third Cross up once more
And, through its power, soon restore
A woman to good health. So they
Are sure they've found Christ's Cross today.

Macarius now lifts on high
The Cross for all to glorify,
And, seeing Christ's True Cross revealed,
The people in repentance kneel.

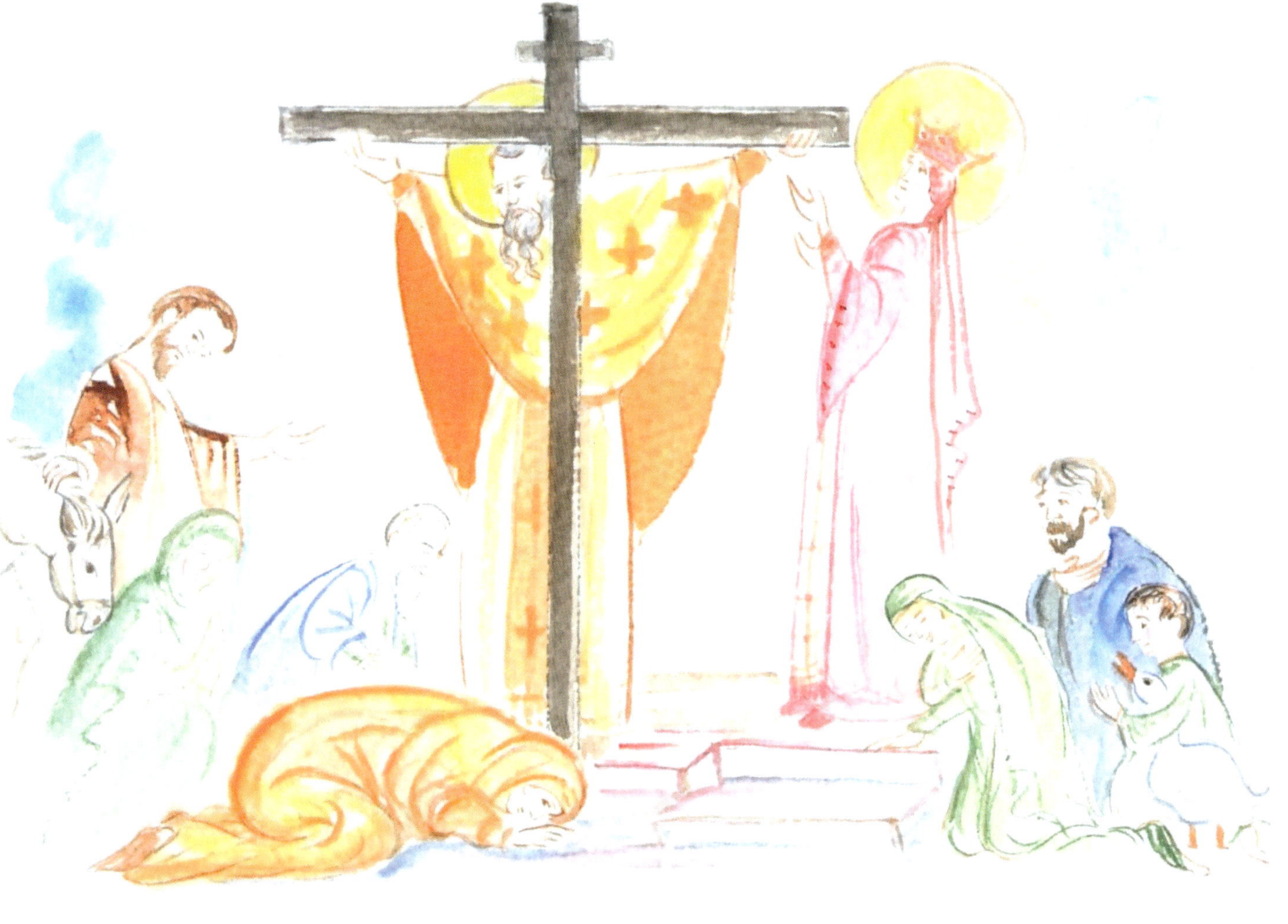

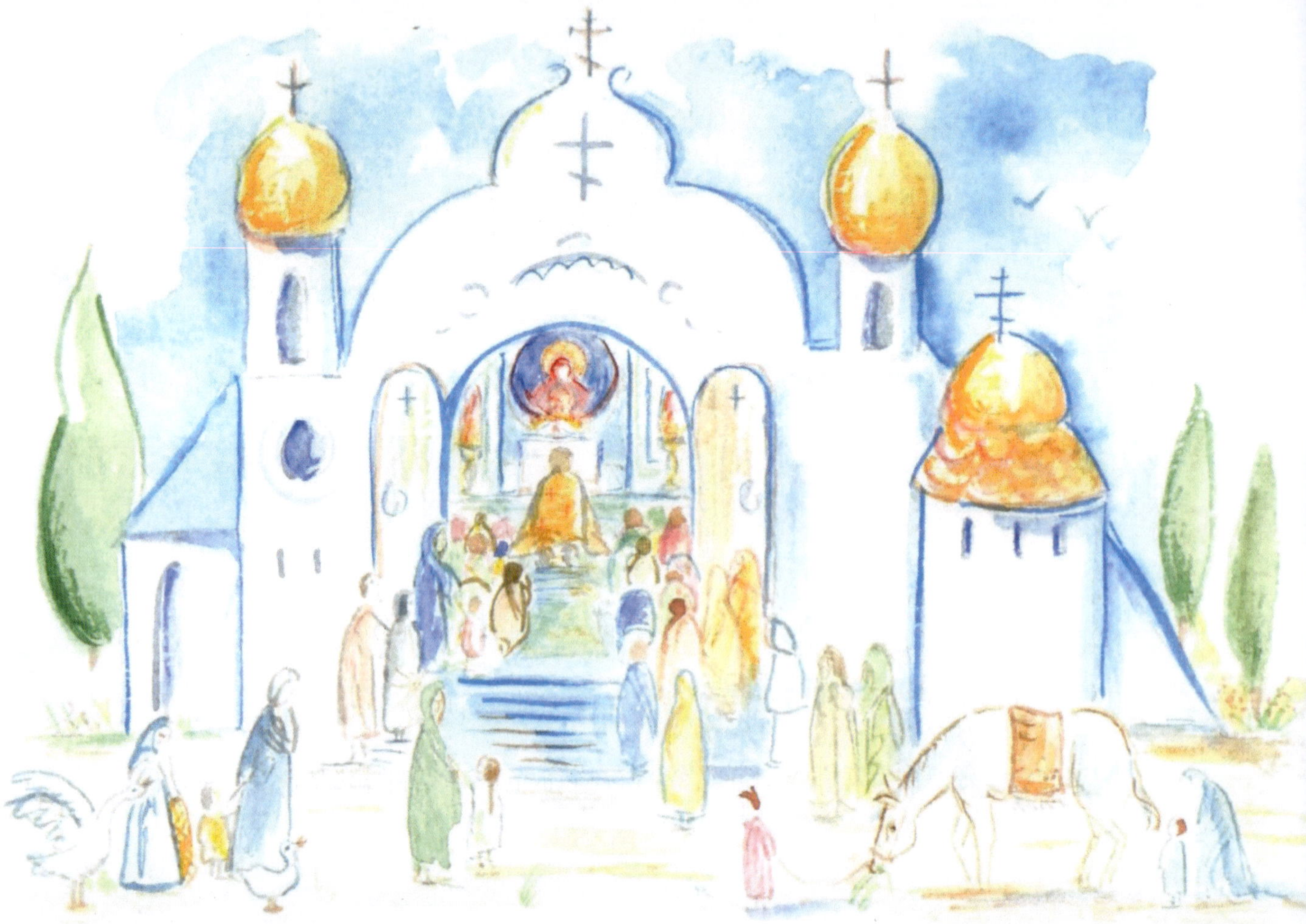

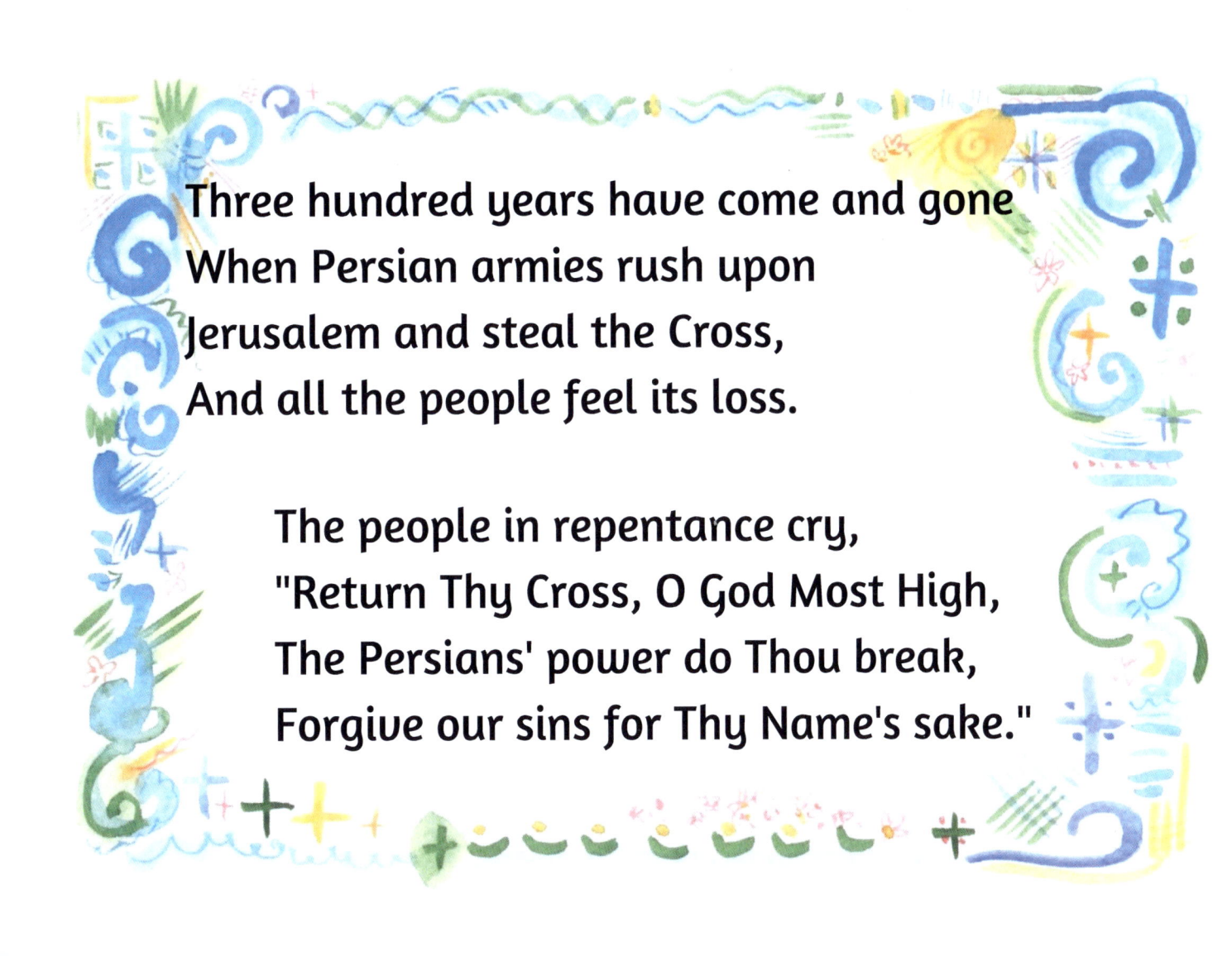

Three hundred years have come and gone
When Persian armies rush upon
Jerusalem and steal the Cross,
And all the people feel its loss.

The people in repentance cry,
"Return Thy Cross, O God Most High,
The Persians' power do Thou break,
Forgive our sins for Thy Name's sake."

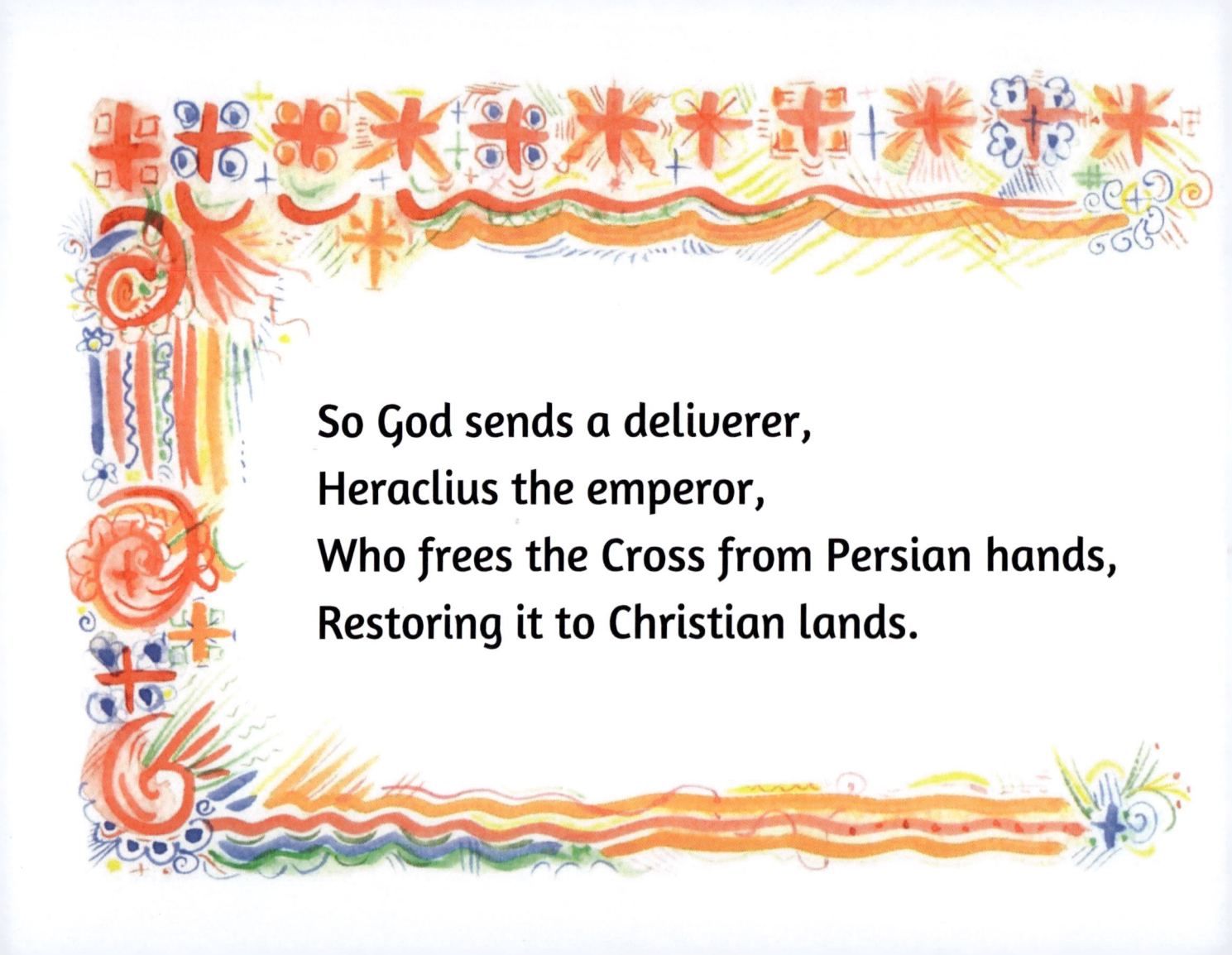

So God sends a deliverer,
Heraclius the emperor,
Who frees the Cross from Persian hands,
Restoring it to Christian lands.

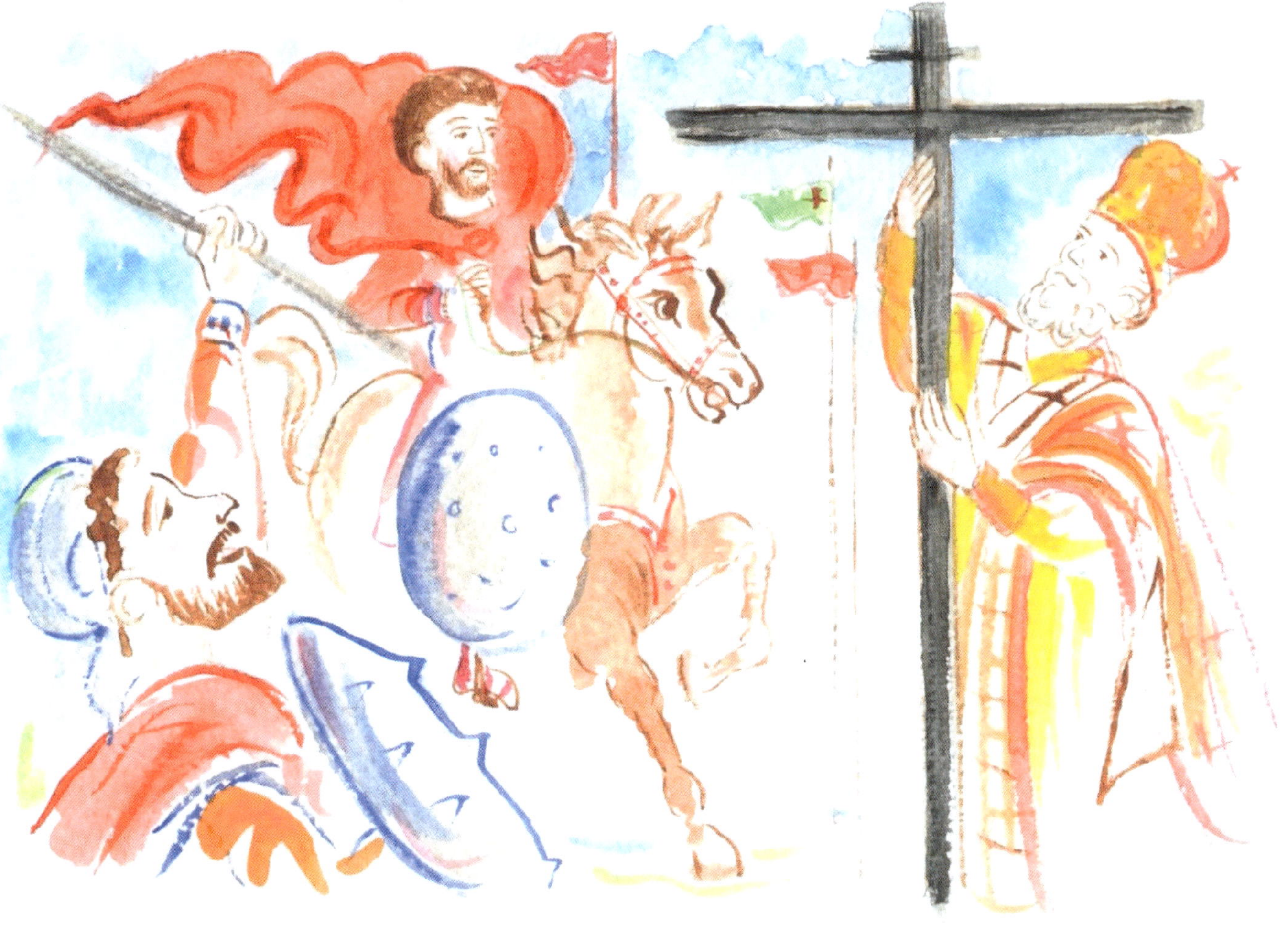

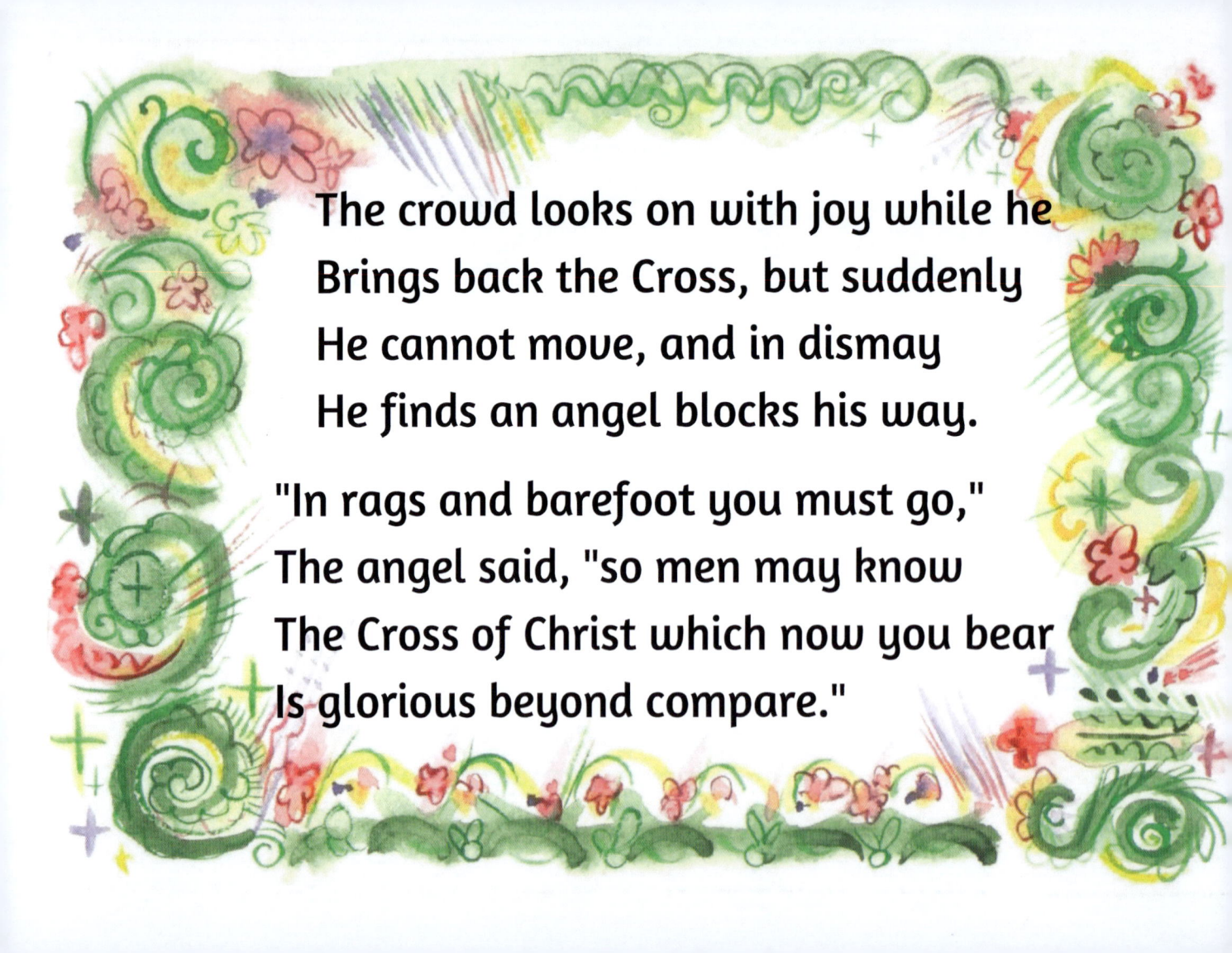

The crowd looks on with joy while he
Brings back the Cross, but suddenly
He cannot move, and in dismay
He finds an angel blocks his way.

"In rags and barefoot you must go,"
The angel said, "so men may know
The Cross of Christ which now you bear
Is glorious beyond compare."

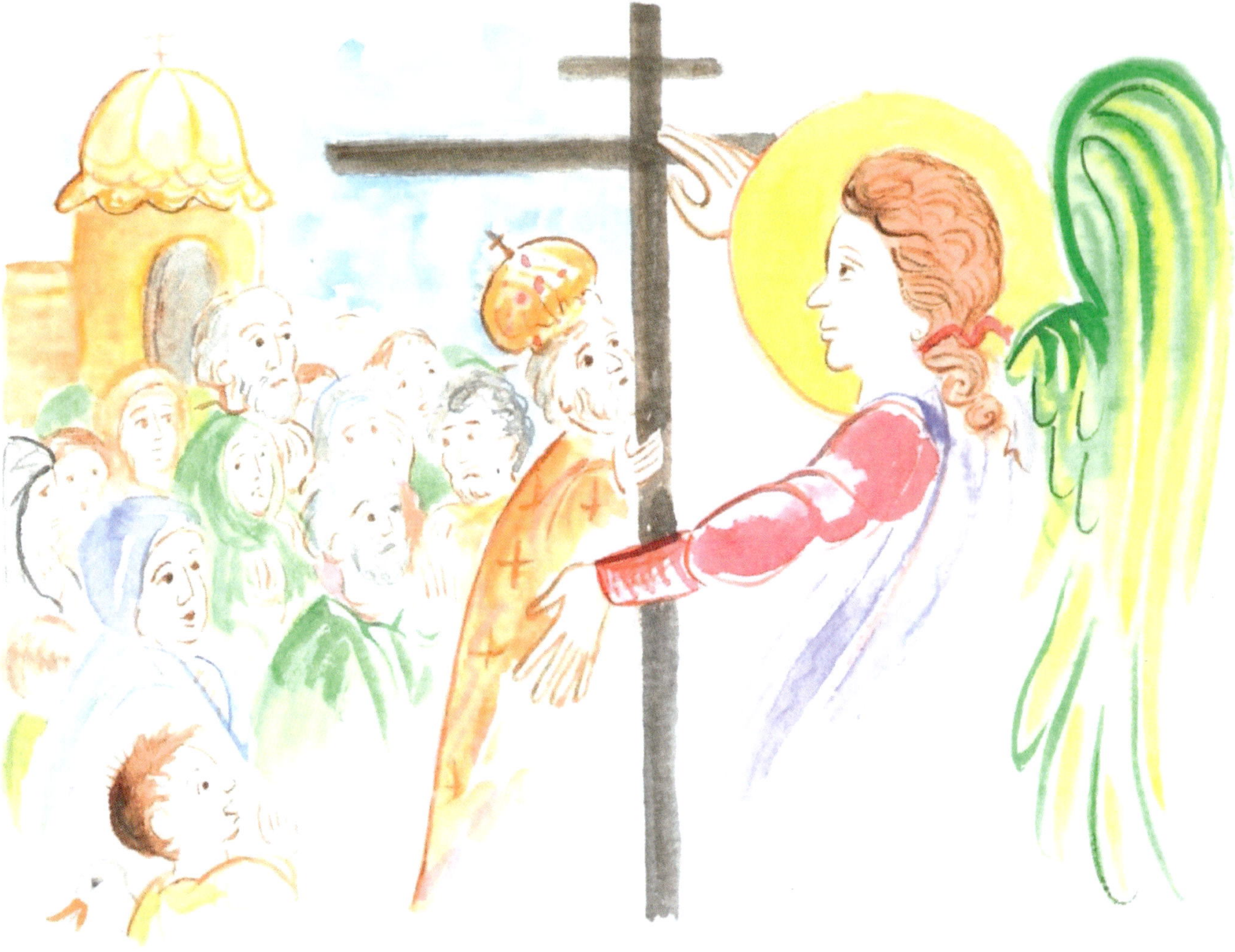

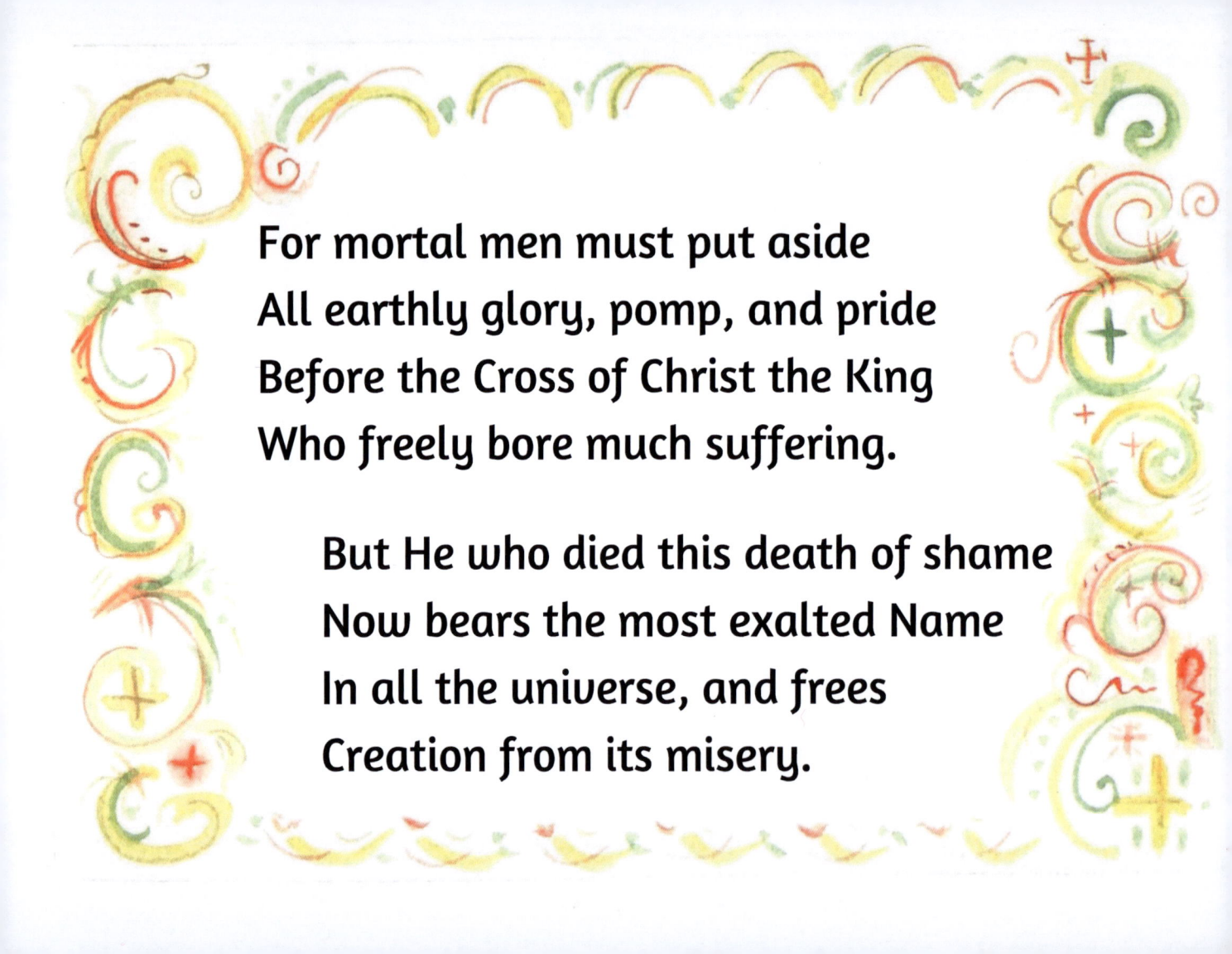

For mortal men must put aside
All earthly glory, pomp, and pride
Before the Cross of Christ the King
Who freely bore much suffering.

But He who died this death of shame
Now bears the most exalted Name
In all the universe, and frees
Creation from its misery.

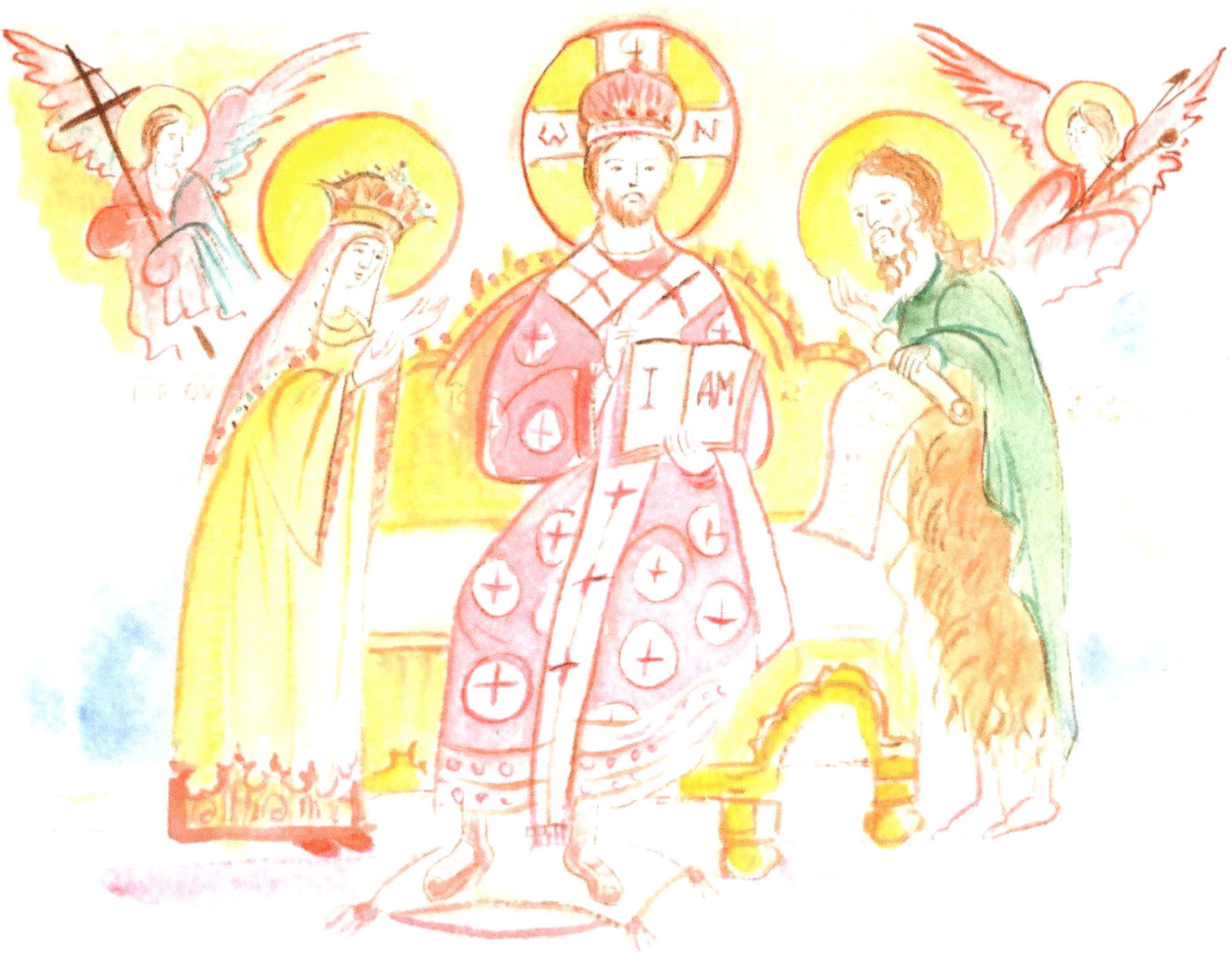

ω
N
I AM

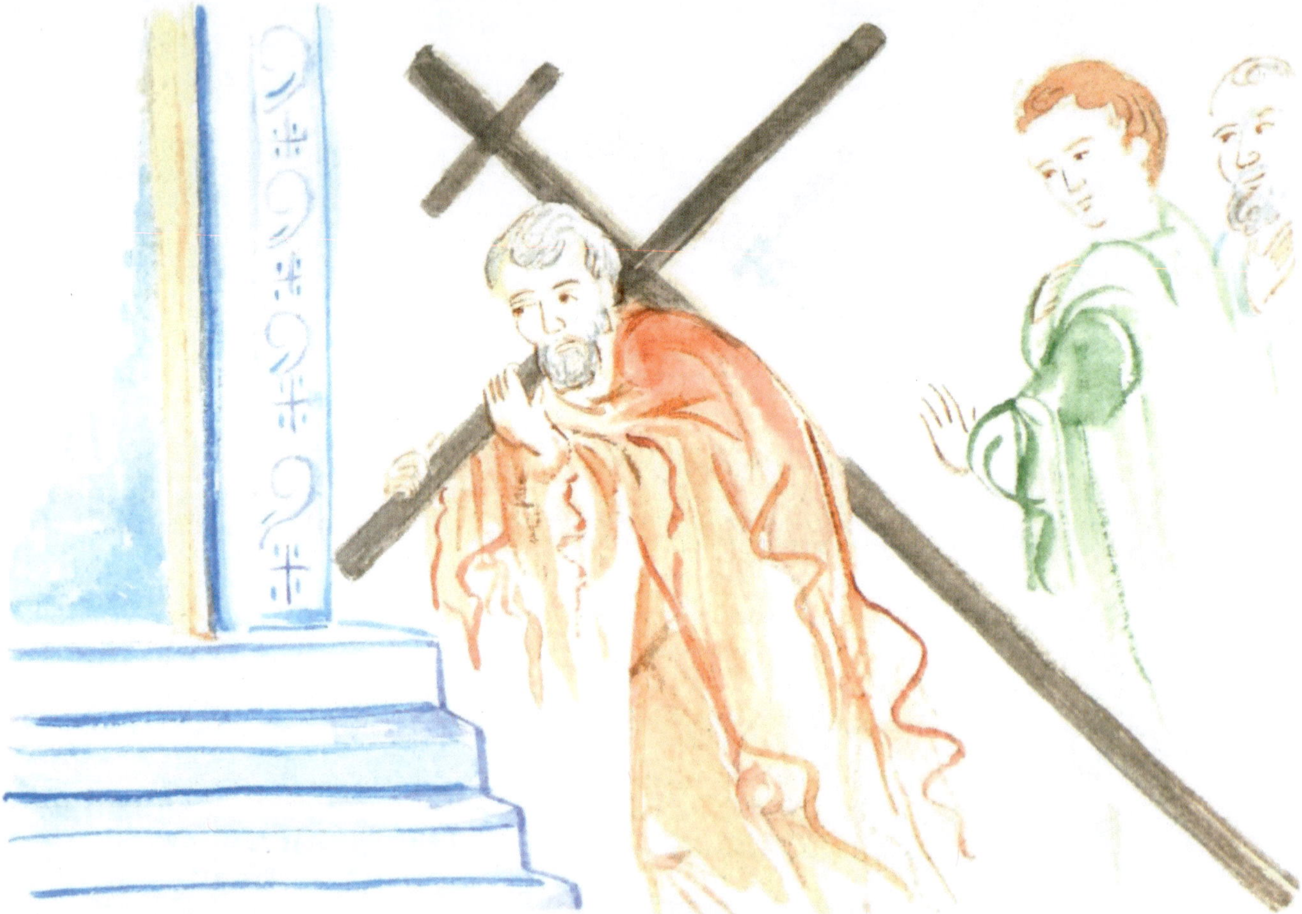

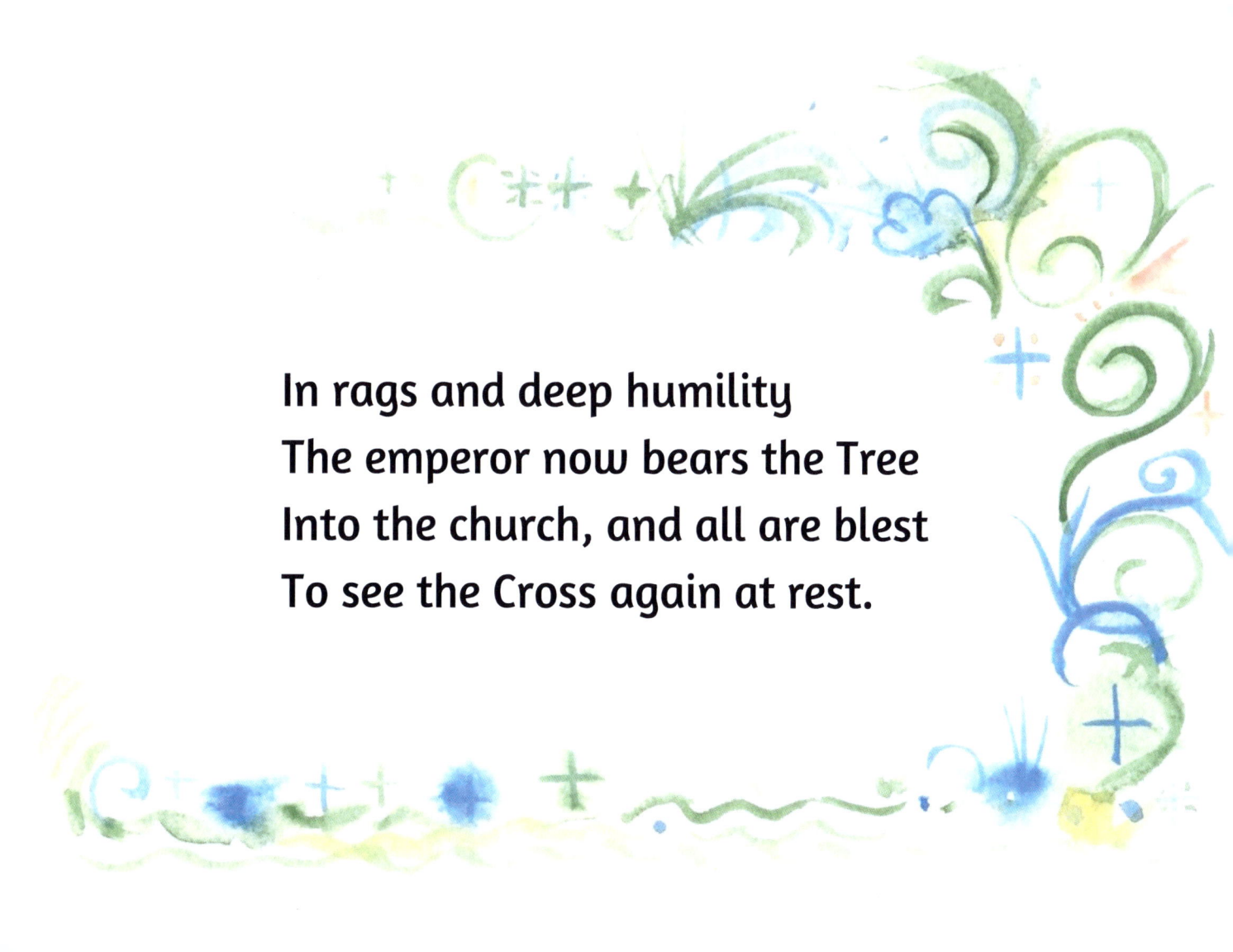

In rags and deep humility
The emperor now bears the Tree
Into the church, and all are blest
To see the Cross again at rest.

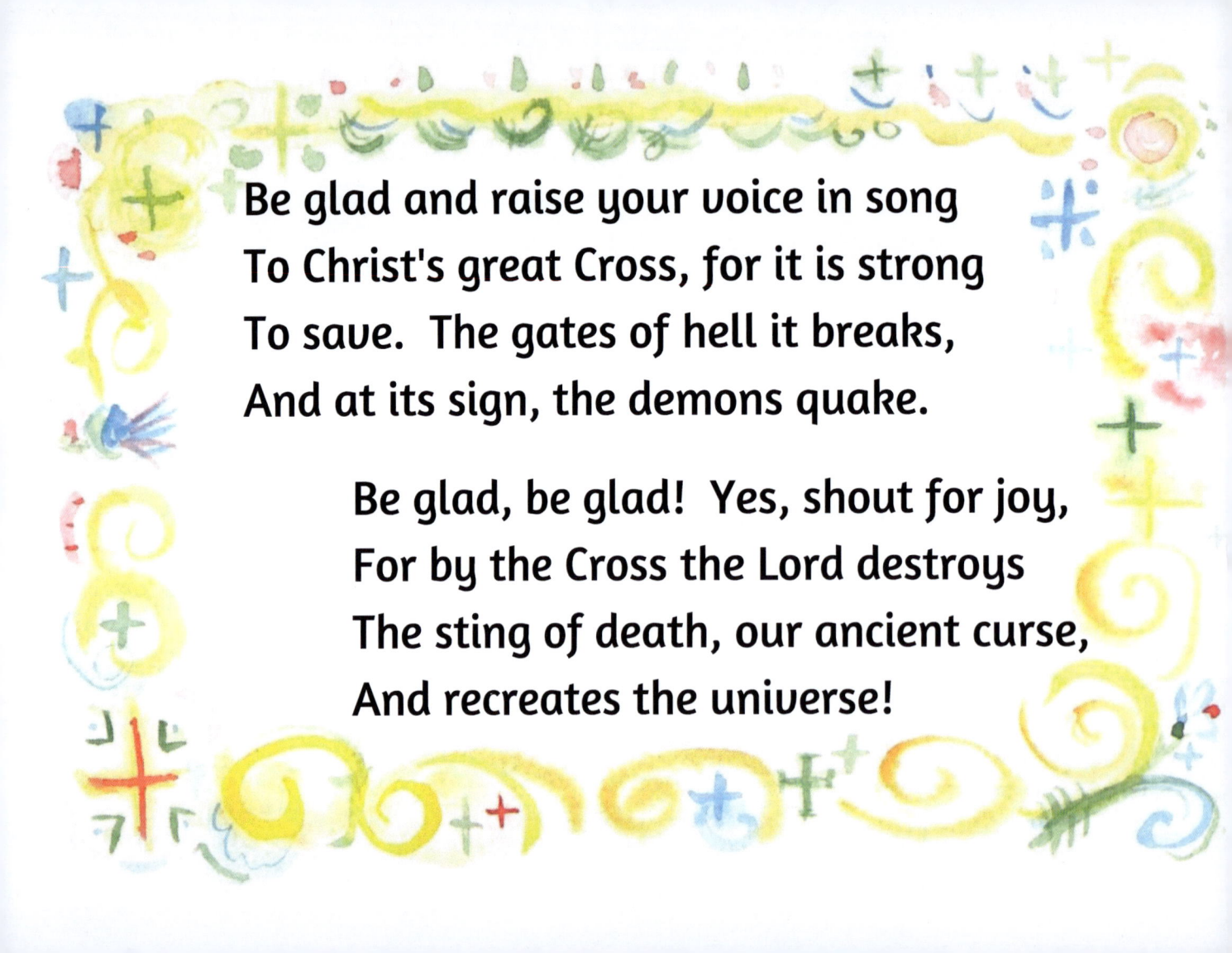

Be glad and raise your voice in song
To Christ's great Cross, for it is strong
To save. The gates of hell it breaks,
And at its sign, the demons quake.

    Be glad, be glad! Yes, shout for joy,
    For by the Cross the Lord destroys
    The sting of death, our ancient curse,
    And recreates the universe!

Check out more of Mother Melania's books.

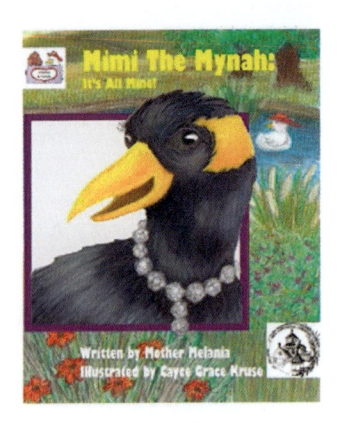

Mimi the Mynah
from

The Fearless & Friends series

Moses and the Burning Bush
from

Old Testament Stories for Children

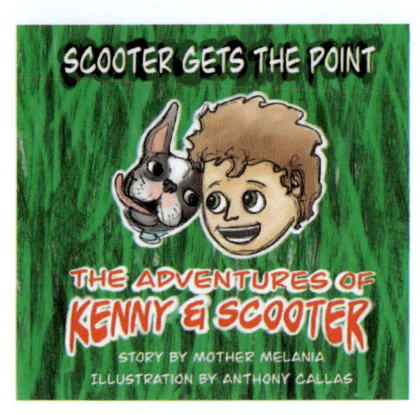

Scooter Gets the Point
from

The Adventures of Kenny & Scooter

Please leave a review on this book's Amazon page—

I'm always looking for feedback from my readers and ways to improve!

Thanks so much, and God bless you!

ABOUT THE AUTHOR AND ILLUSTRATOR

Mother Melania is the abbess of Holy Assumption Monastery in Calistoga, California. She has enjoyed working with children all of her life. In addition to The Twelve Great Feasts series, she has written several other series of children's books, focusing on Scriptural stories and the Paschal cycle, and celebrating the virtues.

Bonnie Gillis is an iconographer and illustrator. She lives in Langley, British Columbia, Canada, where her husband, Father Michael, is pastor of Holy Nativity Orthodox Church.

Printed in Great Britain
by Amazon